Supermarket Service

A Guide to Outstanding Service Success

by Mitchell Lyn

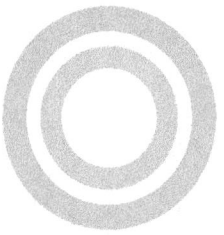

©2020 by the author

Self-published

No part of this publication may be reproduced, stored in a retrieval system, or transmitted in any form or by any means, electronic, mechanical, photocopying, recording, scanning, or otherwise, except as permitted under Section 107 or 108 of the 1976 United States Copyright Act, without either the prior written permission of the Author, or authorization through payment of the appropriate per-copy fee to Mitchell Lyn. Contact the author at MLGodandSouls@gmail.com.

Acknowledgements

Dad, you made it all possible. We miss you, but you live within us.

Contents

Introduction 1

Before We Begin Our Store Tour 7

The Entry 15

Deli/Meat Market 23

Produce 35

Dairy 49

Refreshments 57

Frozen Foods 67

Consumer Packaged Goods 75

Checkout 83

Paper or Plastic? 95

Summary 103

Closing Stories 115

Introduction

Service today—we just don't expect much, do we? Many businesses give their service providers fancy names—sales associates, customer service representatives, guest specialists, etc. Unfortunately, it seems that the customer service often fails to live up to what the name tags suggest.

In today's world, we expect mediocre service and put up with poor service. Any business or person that provides slightly above mediocre service will differentiate themselves, and any business or person that provides superior service will stand out as "the" place to go—good news and bad news travels fast via word of mouth, but mediocre news typically isn't spread.

In addition, today's world of easy and fast internet purchasing makes it very difficult for brick and mortar stores to compete. Mediocre service brings your ability to compete down even more.

But I believe local stores aren't dead. People can check before they buy, they still have to eat, they need haircuts and they often need to try things on. So read on, keep people coming to your store and provide the best possible service.

This book is about service the way it ought to be (or maybe the way it "used to be"—I'm getting old!). It contains nothing magical, just common-sense service ideas from my youth, when my father and his father before, ran a successful supermarket. Their success came during times when big box supermarkets were coming in and selling items at lower perceived prices, when big discount chains began selling absolutely everything in their superstores, and when convenience stores with their self-service allowed people to make quick stops to pick up their snacks instead of going to the supermarket. What made Dad's store so successful? His service! To this day, I meet people from my hometown who remember the store and want to talk about my dad or my 5-foot-tall grandmother who worked as hard as anyone!

My father was an interesting person. He always paid his bills, and I don't think he had an enemy in the world. A few people took advantage of his generosity and trusting nature, but he spread what is truly good to everyone he met. He always had a smile and a great sense of humor, and was particularly known for giving as much grief to, as well as getting it from just about everyone. In today's world, many people tend to think that their job is so important or that they are so busy that they can't take time to have a bit of fun. Dad's life and work suggested that you take time to laugh—laugh at yourself, laugh with others, and never say anything nasty. A good sense of humor makes everyone more comfortable, makes the work at hand more fun and people more productive. Try it!

This book is not meant to be a high-level educational course on service. It is meant to give you the ideas you can draw on, using your own techniques and creativity, to make your job or business a service success. We will take the fifty plus years of customer service experience that Bernie's has and roll them into a few key service points. It is up to you to take over from there.

In this book we take a trip through the supermarket. Sure, you've been to the grocery store many times, but have you taken a look at what really makes a good store work? As we tour the departments, we'll talk about how good service really works, and how you can use the practical tips to help you or your business provide the best possible service.

I hope you find this both practical and educational. The key is to look at what is said, think about how you or your business can change, and bring new ideas to work with you. If you can make some changes and improve your service, you'll be heads above your competition.

Finally, if you have some service suggestions of your own, please let me know! I'd love to take what you have learned and use it to help others. Please email me at Mitch@MitchellLyn.com. Thanks!

Most important, make every day a great day, stay positive, and enjoy reading *Supermarket Service*!

Before We Begin Our Store Tour

Bernie's Supermarket. It doesn't sound like much and in reality, it wasn't much. This small supermarket, located in the heart of Cedar Falls, Iowa probably didn't have annual sales equal to what some of the huge chain stores sell in a week. It was located on a 1.5-acre lot on a relatively busy street, without many other businesses located nearby. There were no large storefronts, chain discount stores, fancy lit parking lots, multiple service center areas, or any of the other large market amenities. The store had two relatively large aisles, plus a deli/meat market, and a large refreshment room. It pales in comparison to where nearly everyone in today's world shops.

Bernie's was a local success story. The store didn't sell anything you couldn't buy at other supermarkets. It wasn't more modern or fancier than other places, and it was maybe the last place to get an electronic cash register! Its success was due to the quality of service given to customers and staff. In this book, we are going to take a walk around the store to visit various departments. Each department had its own set of rules or "laws."

The service laws are what this book is all about. For us, they were the laws we had to abide by. Dad was a very pleasant person, and we never challenged him on these. For you, it is your choice. Because of that, I'm going to call these the "Staples of Good Service."

The Layout

Bernie's was a typical small independent supermarket. There was not a lot of variety of each type of product, and there were not huge quantities of each product carried. I think the cereal section of some of today's supermarkets probably would have covered one whole aisle at Bernie's!

As customers walked up to the store, they first noticed items outside. These were typically seasonal products that attracted attention to the store. They may also have noticed that the store was always neat and clean, with a beautiful storefront.

I remember my grandmother, who worked into her 70's, often wandering outside of the store so she could pick up any papers that had blown into the lot, push carts back into the store, or scoop up trash someone had left behind.

As customers walked through the doors, they were greeted with a sincere smile, and asked if they could be helped in any way. Our goal was to make the first impressions as good as possible.

The store consisted of wide aisles, a meat market/deli, a large refreshment room, and candies and snacks up front. The layout was very important to Dad, as it is to many supermarket owners. First, customers would go by the pharmaceuticals, then down a consumer-packaged goods aisle with all of the canned foods, cereals, and most other foods with a longer shelf life. Towards the back of the aisle were the salty snacks and a rather large pet food section. In the very back of the store was a large meat section with fresh and frozen meats, fresh homemade salads (mostly) and a large deli section. This was followed by the produce area. Another aisle consisted of the dairy section, then frozen foods on the right, and the paper goods and cookies on the left. Finally, the refreshment room was a very large room with cold and warm soda (pop to us Iowans!) and beer. Near the checkout were the cigarettes, individual frozen snacks candy, and magazines.

Store layout was important to Bernie's, as it should be to any business. A term I've called

"Customer Viewpoint Analysis" or CVA in part stems from the layout of the store. Customer viewpoint analysis means not only asking your customers what is important, but just standing back and looking at your business through your customers' eyes. From a layout perspective, it is important to check the store layout as a business owner and a customer.

In Dallas, there was an electronics superstore. Customers walked in from the parking lot to the hub of a wheel shaped store. In the center is a large desk with customer service people behind it. Their purpose is to greet incoming customers and ask how they could be of assistance. The customers can then choose to shop on their own or ask for specific help. Each spoke of the "wheel" is a different retail arm. Computers are in one area, stereos in another, appliances in a third, and so on. The owners of this store truly look at how the customers want it laid out. It was probably more costly to set up initially, but it is an amazingly customer friendly store.

The supermarket was laid out very carefully and was periodically changed as needed. When you first walk in, the aspirin and other items are there when your mind is fresh, to get you thinking about items that are often left off a shopping list. Next you walk through the foods that are typically on a shopping list. The items are colorful and laid out in a way that may make you want to purchase a few extra items. Following packaged goods are chips, which people purchase as a larger impulse item, and which one may grab just because they're hungry.

The back of the store is for the items that most people include on their shopping lists. These include meat, milk, and produce. They are placed in the back so you necessarily walk past the rest of the store to allow customers to think of other items they might need.

Toward the checkout, customers are inundated with impulsive buying products, or items that they likely didn't come to the store for. These include cigarettes, candy, ice cream, beer, pop, and magazines. Many of the discount chains and supermarkets today use this technique. Think of a store that doesn't have candy, magazines and soda by the checkout—not many!

Now, we'll begin our tour and go department by department through the store. In detail, we'll discuss different ways each department used "Staples of Good Service" to maintain high service standards. Read on, and get hungry for superior service!

The Entry

The entry to any retail store is the first impression the customer gets. They key to success both in the external view of the store and the entry is to pay attention to the details. A clean entry way, working light bulbs in the signage, a well-maintained entry rug, and a picked-up entry way are all positive reasons for a customer to enter and enjoy their experience.

At Bernie's, people noticed the cleanliness, as they were welcomed into the store and greeted with a smile. The goal was to make the first impression a lasting one.

Our first staple was Bernie's most important, without exception. We were to remember this from the time the customer walked into the entry until they left. We were also to know this staple 24 hours a day, as everyone we met every day, in and out of the store, was a potential customer.

Staple #1: THE CUSTOMER IS ALWAYS RIGHT

Dad daily reminded the staff of his most important staple,

"The customer is always right! Even if the customer isn't always right—the customer is always right!"

Of course, the customer wasn't always right. But we had to make every effort to please every customer and to make every customer feel like we were only in business for them.

Here are some examples:

If a customer complained that their milk was sour, we would replace it—no questions asked.

If a customer wanted a brand other than what we carried, we would let them sample the brands we carried.

If a customer wanted a new product, we would tell Bernie about it.

If the customer gave us a $10 bill and told us it was a twenty, we were always trained to keep the bill on top of the cash drawer until the transaction was complete, so we could show the customer. So although obviously the customer wasn't right, this corrected them without threatening them, and they always went away happy.

And the examples can go on and on . . . .

There are so many businesses that forget to focus on their customers. This doesn't relate only to retail businesses. Everyone has customers. But does everyone define who their customers are (they can be other departments internally, other businesses, individuals, retail customers or any other ways you can define them.)

If you get nothing else from this book:

- Find out who your customers are.
- Find out what your customers want.
- Make your total focus the customer.
- Always let the customer know that they are right.
- Don't ever forget this staple.

In today's world, many people focus on other things. Our lives are spent pulling up information from anywhere in the world, making personal calls, wasting time eating donuts or in corporate meetings for who knows what, arguing with others for who knows why, and who knows how many other distractions. Let's take the time to figure out what is important—our customer, and deliver to them the best possible products and services. If every waiter at every restaurant realized that the paying customer is the reason they have a job, they would make every customer's restaurant experience a great one.

Here is my wish list:

That personal calls no longer exist at any retail store, and that the customer is the focus for every employee.

That business employees quit telling customers to "have a great day," and start truly appreciating the business.

That retail stores are filled with employees who are knowledgeable about their products and what their competitors offer.

That service industry employees keep their customers' best interests in mind when selling services—even if it means sending them elsewhere for the service.

You can add a few more. Think of your favorite place to shop, eat, or do business. Are you the customer that is most important to them? Are you always right in their minds? Are your customers always right?

Staple #2: Enjoy what you do, and let it show through to the customer from the time they set foot in the door.

"Have Fun!"

Regardless of anything else, we could never let the customer know that our experience with that customer was anything but great. We couldn't afford to let any customer know that we didn't enjoy every second of our job. We maintained constant, sincere smiles.

I think this is important all of the time. Life is way too short to not have fun. Those who don't have fun only make themselves miserable. Why think negative thoughts when positive thoughts are so much better for your health and those around you.

For example, do you hold a grudge against anyone? Why? Is it really worth it? Chances are that the person you hold the grudge against probably doesn't even know it, so you only bring yourself down and the other person could probably care less!

A woman works at a clothing retailer. This woman has three young children at home, lost an arm a few years ago in an auto accident, and had a husband who left her for another woman. This woman has a lot to be angry about. Yet at work and at home, she appreciates all that she does have, not what she doesn't. She makes every customer's shopping experience an excellent one by smiling, enjoying the customer and making their shopping experience as fun as possible. She also is like this while outside of work.

Who would you appreciate more as a customer—this woman or the person who thinks that their business owes them a living and customers are a nuisance?

So be happy, enjoy life and your work, whatever it may be.

Deli/Meat Market

The deli and meat market were a favorite of customers and a favorite of Bernie's. It was truly the area that made this store unique from other supermarkets in the area. And when the owner's and customers' favorite departments are the same, I would suggest you make this a showpiece and the center of your business. That's exactly what Bernie did.

If you asked people in Cedar Falls today what their favorite meat market has been, I'm sure many would still answer Bernie's Supermarket. This area was truly unique. I can still sense the great taste of some of the home-made salads. First, and foremost, were Bernie's World-Famous Baked Beans and Bernie's Potato Salad. Both of these salads were made from scratch, and both had that extra bit of flavor that no one except the "chefs" knew about. Additionally, Bernie's was known to have the freshest, best tasting ground beef, great beef and pork cuts, and a large variety of deli meats and cheeses.

Because this was such a strong product line, and people were a bit less cost-conscience about the items. My father focused almost entirely on quality. In other words, if your business offers a unique item with a strong demand, focus less on low pricing and much more on high quality. A good value will keep people coming back and purchasing—not a cheap product.

Staple #3: Make what is truly unique your showpiece.

"Spice the beans, and don't forget to add the secret ingredient to the potato salad!"

The days spent making beans and potato salad were the days of torture. We used to boil pots and pots of potatoes, then would skin and cut them for hours. They were always so hot after boiling, and we would burn our hands until they were done, then we'd crack and cut the hard-boiled eggs! When the potato salad was finally finished, the beans had to be watched carefully and spiced just right. Dad knew of only one way to make the beans—hot and spicy!

The store would go through beans and potato salad by the pints, quarts, and sometimes gallons. People used to tell us how and when they'd eat them, they would let us know that combining the two made a much better combination, and they'd request less spicy beans, but never really wanted that. But also, this was a major key to the business. Once you had Bernie's baked beans and potato salad, you were hooked and couldn't go elsewhere. In fact, about 10 years after I had gone out on my own, I made some of the famous baked beans in northern Minnesota. Believe it or not, I had someone come up to me and tell me how they used to enjoy the beans at Bernie's!

A key to service is to be extremely good at something, do it well, make it right, and be known for it. If Bernie's hadn't offered these world-famous baked beans, it would have been just another supermarket. People would have no reason to drive past their local store to go to Bernie's. The store didn't offer better canned soup than anyone else, the chips were the same, and the ice cream was all cold. It did offer the absolute best beans and potato salad around, and the secrets and special touches made it worth the trip.

Staple #4: Personalize your service to the extent possible.

"Make sandwiches the way the customers want!"

Value, value, value. As a supermarket, we had quite a lunch business on a daily basis. Every weekday during the noon hour, lines of people would come to pick up their sandwiches, potato salad, chips, pop, and cupcakes. They would also stand around the store, read magazines, talk a lot with each other and with our staff, and have a great, fast-food style lunch hour. We were not a fast food restaurant, but we did make sandwiches the way our customers wanted them. We'd give them the kind of bread they wanted, their choice of meats or cheeses, and whatever toppings they wanted. The rest of the lunch was purchased off the shelf.

What made it work? We knew our customers, and would make sandwiches fresh in the morning, and actually put the customer's name on the sandwich. In addition, my father taught us how to pile the lunchmeats in such a way as to make the sandwich look much, much larger than just placing the meat on flat. The sandwiches were prepared truly the way the customer wanted them.

How well do you truly know your customers? Do you do what it takes in your off time to personalize goods and services for your customers? Do you look for special products or purchases that might benefit your customer, and call them about it? How about taking a regular product and packaging it in a way that makes it appear to be a better value? These things can be money makers for you and a benefit to your customer.

As an example, I went to a retail store the other day to look for a gift for some friends. The clerk showed me some pasta serving ware, which looked fine in a box. The cost was $35.00. She then showed me a package that was already cellophane wrapped, which included the pasta serving ware, out of the box in a basket, two bottles of fine oil, and matching cloth napkins. She told me they didn't charge for the wrapping, and the total of the goods came to $59.00! Guess which one I bought? I spent a little more, but I didn't have to wrap the gift, and I gave a very nice gift to our friends. Although this wasn't specifically personalized to me, the store would have done that, and I still came away with a gift that cost a bit more, but had much more value to me than just the box of pasta serving ware!

Staple #5: Business integrity is all about cleanliness.

"Always wash your hands when working with meat!"

In fact, everything was kept as clean as possible at Bernie's. Dad always felt that cleanliness, as well as perceived cleanliness, was so important to maintaining integrity with our customers. Without question, cleanliness was of utmost importance.

Did Bernie have to keep everything as clean as possible? No! People wouldn't have noticed. What he did, though, was to incorporate integrity into the business. He never self-promoted the cleanliness; it was just an important part of the operations that was not compromised under any circumstance.

Integrity is the key to this staple. I suggest that the businesses today who truly offer the highest quality service do so with integrity. Any person or business that runs without integrity is doomed to fail eventually.

Another important point about cleanliness—perceived cleanliness is also important. Even though you might know that what you are doing is ok, the customer may not know that.

For example, every time we waited on a customer in the deli and meat market, we would ask them to wait a second while we washed our hands. Our hands may have been very clean already, but perceived cleanliness . . . .

Is your place of business as clean as possible? Is smoking allowed? Do people trust that you do what you can to make it as pleasant of an environment as possible? Do you have old items sitting around? My advice is to wash your hands, pick up, and keep the place clean. Your customers will know, and you will feel a whole lot better!

Cleanliness was important throughout the store. We kept the duster in the front, and continually dusted when not busy. Every night at the store, the floor was swept and mopped right after closing. We paid attention to every detail.

Finally, clean white aprons were worn by every employee while on duty. These not only gave the appearance of cleanliness, they also differentiated the staff from customers, so customers new to the store could easily figure out who to ask questions of.

I once did some consulting work for an auto dealer. The customer focus groups told us they wanted the dealership kept clean and smoke free vehicles as well as facility. This was not a dirty dealership, but they did allow smoking in the building, and they had some parts sitting near some sales offices for a few months.

We suggested getting rid of the clutter and making the establishment and vehicles non-smoking. We also recommended that the used cars be cleaned completely, and the smoke smell removed to the extent possible. The last step was to educate the market about their new methods and their cleanliness. Just by doing that alone, business increased by 25% over the subsequent six months, even though business was good prior to that!

Pay attention to the details. And for everyone, everywhere—when you are not busy with other things, clean!

Produce

Strong memories to our senses often come back to us throughout our lives. Do you remember that special song that you and your first romantic interest shared together? How about a particular smell of something wonderful, like lilacs in the spring? The unexpected feeling the first time you touched a snake . . . . Ordinary daily activities or senses typically don't stand out, like the taste of milk or a song you heard on the way to work yesterday morning.

The produce section was an area where all senses are affected. Customers want produce that smells great, looks colorful and fresh, is just right to the touch, sounds good when you thump it and, of course, tastes great at home without being over or under ripe.

Produce is where the color is, and most people can easily identify with good, fresh produce. I always felt we spent too much time in displaying the produce, but Bernie thought that good produce, although not a money maker in itself (too much spoilage), brings people to the store to buy their other groceries. Fruits and vegetables are an end-point item. This, healthy or not, means that people don't typically come to the store for another item, then decide impulsively to purchase fruits and vegetables. They are usually on the customer's shopping list and a reason to go to the store.

According to The Collins Dictionary and Thesaurus, produce is defined as:

- vb. to bring into existence
- vb. to make
- vb. to give birth to
- vb. to present to view
- vb. to bring before the public
- n. anything produced
- n. agricultural products collectively

To produce is to bring into existence or to make, for those manufacturers, or to present to view or bring before the public to retailers. This is a key to great service.

Staple #6: Become known for providing a good value to the customer.

"The season is the reason that the price is nice!"

This doesn't say always be the cheapest. Almost contrary to that, giving great service means giving great value. In other words, customers were willing to pay a higher price, within reason, for much higher quality. We purchased fruit only at trusted wholesalers, and sent back anything that wasn't top quality. Even if something looks good, if a customer brings fruit home and finds it spoiled or not tasting good, they may tell their friends and they may not return.

We would only stock fruit in season. If it was out of season, chances are it was not that good or too high priced. If it was in-season and high quality, we could sell it for a decent price and make some money doing so.

Think about your produce—the things that customers come to your store for specifically or the items on their "grocery lists." Is it a good value to the customer? Does it always look good? If not, what can you do to make it better? I'm keen on sales and marketing, as I have spent many years in that field, but marketing a product that isn't a good value to the customer is simply a waste of money in the long run.

Writing this chapter on produce does bring back old, painful memories (produce was probably my least favorite section!) I used to dread the days that the semi-full of watermelons stopped in. I was thankful for dad's pickiness about quality, for he often turned the truck away without purchasing, but on the days he purchased . . . I, being the strongest, always had the honor of catching the watermelons that were thrown off the truck by the driver. I'd toss them to dad, and he would stack them. My younger brother had the difficult job of making sure they were stacked all right! Some days, I'm sure we unloaded four or five tons of watermelons that way.

How picky are you that your customer is getting a good value for their dollar?

Staple #7: Make your products appealing to the customer.

"Keep produce looking fresh!"

In the produce section, with every case of individual fruit, like apples or pears, we would polish each piece of fruit, toss the not so good stuff back into the box, and display the good fruit individually. At Bernie's, we didn't have sprayers to make the produce look wet, but we did clean it all so the customer could pick up fruit and eat it—right after they purchased it! Fresh 100% pure ground beef was what was advertised and what was sold at Bernie's. At a time when other supermarkets may have included livers, hearts and unmentionable parts in their hamburger, Bernie's ground up only fine beef, with just a touch of the trimmed fat remaining so it would grill up nicely. No shortcuts were allowed on any of the meats. Steaks were typically cut fresh, particularly when we started buying rib eye and sirloin in bulk, rather than beef halves. The meat was good, and had to look good.

So here's the tip—if you want to sell a product, make it look as good as you possibly can.

An example of how this works well is in the used automobile business. Think of the last time you went car shopping. This is a huge purchase for most people. You were probably excited to test drive a few cars. You knew the style and size you wanted, and when you saw the car, you knew right away that this was the car for you! Why? Likely because the car was cleaned inside and the polish made it shine like a new car. Compare this to going to a dealer who has dirty cars that they don't touch up at all. A little bit of effort into making and keeping your products looking good is an important service to customers.

Staple #8: Be the expert on your products and the competition.

"Know how to pick out a fresh cantaloupe or watermelon!"

Have you ever thumped a watermelon, squeezed a pear, smelled an orange, or eyed an apple? What are you looking for? At Bernie's, we would be right there to help you. Most people are not experts at every subject, and most people probably don't know as much about your products or services as you do. So, if you're going to be in the business, be the best at what you do.

At Bernie's, we knew everything we could about the products we sold, including memorizing most of the prices and having answers to our customers questions. We couldn't always beat our competitors in size or price, but we felt we were much better than them in product knowledge and service. We knew what products our competitors were selling and at what prices. We knew as much as possible about our products, including when fruits and vegetables were at their peak. We knew how to operate all the equipment to best serve the customers. And mostly, we knew that if we didn't know, we were to say so. Dad felt that we should know as much as possible, but we should never, ever lie or mislead the customer.

Are you the best at what you do?

Staple #9: Listen to every customer.

"Corn comes on ears and potatoes have eyes, but no produce has a mouth!"

Dad used to say, "God made us with two ears and two eyes, but only one mouth. Use them in that proportion."

Ok, ok . . . this is a bit of a stretch for the produce department! I had to fit in a spot for listening and observing skills. We used to have it beaten into our heads the importance of always paying attention to the customers' needs. Call me old-fashioned, but I'm still of the school of thought that says the best sales people are consultants—they listen to your needs, help decide on what the problems are, and consult with you in coming to a means for overcoming those problems, even if it may not result in a sale.

Sweet corn is an example of product knowledge. We knew that sweet corn is best when purchased (and eaten) the day it is picked. So in season, we would purchase fresh sweet corn each morning from reputable farmers, and would only purchase what we thought would sell. When a new corn customer came to make a purchase, we would show them how to tell corn that was ready to eat versus corn that wasn't quite done. We would tell them the best ways to prepare the corn, if they were interested, and we would open up each ear of corn to show them how good it was. The excess ears were tossed each night. We knew corn and our customers were loyal to whom they purchased from.

Here are a few examples of improving your listening skills and trying to know your customer better. I suggest you brainstorm to come up with as many ways as possible, then go over your list and this one to come up with ways of improving your customer communication skills.

Always respond to your messages within 4 business hours.

Ask your customers what their needs are. This includes individually, in focus groups, through questionnaires and other research, and through community involvement.

When speaking to a customer, focus only on that customer. Other things are not important at that point in time.

Always make your customer feel important and thank them for input.

Use the customer's name whenever possible. If you are just learning their name, repeat it three or more times during the first conversation to attempt to remember it.

Be honest with the customer. Lies or immoral behavior will get you nowhere fast.

Have fun, and smile. Nothing is worse than dealing with a service person having a bad day.

Walk through your business as a customer, and view all the details that a customer might see—are you happy with what you see. Better yet, have friends or consultants do this for you. This, as a paid service, will easily pay for itself in many cases.

Listen to every customer, regardless of what they buy.

Dairy

Whole milk, 2%, 1%, skim, sweet acidophilus, soymilk, cheeses, eggs and so much more that virtually everyone who entered the store purchased items from this section. The problem is, milk spoils and cheese gets moldy, so how do you keep it fresh?

The dairy section was probably the one we were most creative about loading up. We liked to keep the coolers full, as it made the products appear fresher. Why I don't know, but a cooler with low inventory did look horrible. The creativity came with how to carry cases of dairy products from the walk-in cooler to the dairy case with the least amount of effort. The cases in themselves were manageable, but carrying multiple cases was a job. I tended to be a carrier, dad and my brother used a two-wheeler and my sisters liked to carry milk out by the carton, and make many trips. The one lesson we were taught was:

Staple #10: The best ways to sell more of a commodity is to be better liked or to provide a better presentation.

"Keep the dairy coolers full!"

A full milk case captures your attention and makes customers want to look for items to purchase. Keeping the case full and checking it frequently ensured that the case is attractive and clean. We would clean the milk that leaked from the containers, pull off any items that were outdated, move old stock forward and make sure in general the case looked appealing and attractive. Dairy products were our highest turnover and a relatively low margin product. Because milk and other dairy products are basically commodities, the only way to make money is to sell more—assuming you make money on each product. The only way to sell more of a commodity is to be better liked or provide a better presentation.

If you sell a high turnover commodity type of product, how can you differentiate from your competition? For example, insurance is insurance is insurance. I have not been one who is much into pricing insurance, and if I was, what would make one company's insurance on my car worth $1,000 per year if another company's identical type of insurance is $1,800? For me, I found an agent I trust. I can call him when I have a problem, and he makes sure I'm taken care of. He calls me periodically for a check up on my insurance, and I look at coverage, not cost. I go to him because he is convenient and gives good service, not because of the product he offers. Work on differentiating yourself from your competition.

Do things better than everyone else, and enjoy the benefits.

As another example, think of the lowest priced discount store in your community. Do they get l00% of the business in the area for all the products they sell? I can assure you that is not the case. There are many reasons people will pay a higher price for the same or similar products—including convenience, service, location, ambiance and more. Work on ways to check your dairy case to keep customers wanting more product.

Staple #11: Check your inventory regularly for defects or wear.

"Cracked eggs scramble customer service!"

Humpty Dumpty had a great fall and they couldn't put him back together again. Next to a broken jar of pickles or baby food, broken eggs are about the worst thing to clean up. Most of the time, eggs were fine. Periodically, we would run into an egg purchase where some of the shells were extremely soft. Then, it seemed like some would break just by opening the carton! We did check every dozen eggs we sold—twice. The first time was when we placed them on the shelf. The second, when we could, was when the customer was purchasing them.

Why would we check the eggs? Why wouldn't we check the eggs? We wanted to show that every detail was paid great attention. Some of the large entertainment companies you know of pride themselves on their attention to detail. They don't want any guests in their stores or theme parks to see anything that might make their visit a bad one. Characters are to always act according to the strictest character standards, and are only allowed to come out of character when they are for certain behind the scenes. In the same way, if someone gets one bad egg when they take their groceries out of the bag, they might consider their shopping experience a bad one.

Spoiled milk is horrible, and another reason to check for defects or wear. Once in a blue moon, a customer would return a dairy item because it was spoiled, and usually that was because it was not sealed properly. We made every effort to prevent this. Usually, when a customer called that their milk was spoiled, we would offer to hand deliver a new carton of milk, and would typically throw in something extra for the inconvenience. In order to be the best at service, we had to admit to our mistakes, and do the best we could to keep customers with spoiled milk as long term customers.

How do you handle milk complaints? Do you make it miserable for customers, or do you take a periodic hit, but let the customer know that they are always right? Do you simply return an item with a grumble, or do you smile, make it simple, apologize, then thank the customer for their business and give them something extra? At Bernie's, we didn't cry over spoiled milk!

Think of how frustrating it is to walk into a place of business and see that the details are not being paid attention to. What if someone is on a personal phone conversation and not paying attention to you? What if you find dust on some of the products, or small products broken or cracked? What if a salesperson tells you that they don't have the presentation completed yet, or they waste your time because they weren't prepared with the details?

Look at your eggs. What little things can you check to make sure that every customer's experience with you is a good one?

Refreshments

There weren't many convenience stores near Bernie's Supermarket. Convenience stores, almost by definition, are higher priced than a supermarket is. And, if minimum wage-earning staff who aren't well enough trained to be as fast and efficient as possible are the norm for these businesses, they aren't even convenient. So, if you can't compete on price, convenience, location or service, what's left?

Bernie's understood that some customers valued their time as most important in the equation of where to shop for groceries. Customers in a hurry could stop in, purchase an item without waiting in a long line and leave within a matter of a literally a few seconds. And price? Although not the cheapest in town, Bernie's made it a practice to always be competitive on price. Dad always felt it was better to price fairly and make a little off a lot of people, than to gouge some people and have loss for others. This was most apparent in one of the most "convenience store" areas—the refreshment section.

Because this was a money maker, and many people stopped in for beer and soda, this was also a huge section for the store. The refreshment area was right up front, with a large beer room and a larger soda room.

Staple #12:   If selection is important to your customers, be "top of mind" by providing the largest selection.

"If they want it, we've got it!"

It didn't really matter what kind of refreshments people purchased at Bernie's, as long as Bernie's was the place people turned to in order to buy refreshments. So a point was made to offer as much variety as possible, to give people the option to purchase either in prepared size packages (six packs, cases, etc.) or individually (just like sandwiches), and to offer products both warm and cold.

A convenience factor for customers was putting soda machines in front of the store. By doing so, we had 24-hour sales and took the transactions out of the store. The machines were supplied by the vendors for free, so all we had to do was keep the change filled, collect the money, and stock the machines. Quite easy and profitable!

How can you make your services more convenient to customers? Think of what you can do to take away the high volume, low (or no) income transactions from staff, and become more automated. I am not suggesting automation is always good. If it is easy for your customers and saves you time and money, it is probably worth considering. If it is automation just for the sake of automation, consider what good it will really do you.

When it came to "top of mind" awareness for beer and soft drinks, Bernie's was the number one choice. Do you know who the number one choice is in your market? It is a good idea to do a survey of your market to find out what is important to customers, and how you rate in what is important to your customers. Bernie's found that having the right type of beer or soda was important to their customers. So instead of filling up the rooms with a pre-chosen variety of certain kinds that may or may not be popular, he allowed each of the vendors to put a variety of drinks in their sections. This gave customers the ability to decide what was and wasn't important to stock. If an item was successful, an inventory was maintained. If it was not successful, it was no longer stocked.

What products do you showcase? Do you let the customer decide what's important or do you make that decision? I remember a store of a very large discount retailer that opened up in a community I once lived in. At the opening, members of the community were invited to attend. During the celebration, the manager of the store stood up to address everyone. He told us that although this was the opening of the store, it was the worst inventory they were going to have from then on. He went on to explain that their goal was to find out from the customers what was important in the local market, and to stock the important items and pull off the shelves things that were not in demand. In other words, this one store of a large chain was going to do what it took to learn about its customers and provide the variety that the market wanted, not what the national headquarters requested. He also stated that he would always be open to reviewing and selling locally produced items. He couldn't guarantee they would sell them, or that they would be sold nationally, but he was open to all requests.

How can you provide what your customers want? Do you have showcase items that draw people to do business with you? Do you offer the variety that your customers need, and are you open for suggestions and willing to change?

Staple #13: Price fairly.

"Don't make them pop for pop!"

Price is a difficult thing in the refreshments area. Do you ever go into a convenience store to purchase soda or coffee? My good friend suggests that coffee doesn't really have a value. It truly is whatever the seller feels like charging. To prove the point, try filling your own cup up at a variety of different coffee servers. I can almost guarantee that you will be charged as many different prices as places you go to, that the prices will range from everything from free to $1.00 per cup or more, and that the price likely has nothing to do with the quality of the cup of coffee! I travel quite a bit and I drink quite a bit of coffee, so I do take note of who charges what and I only buy my coffee at the shops with the best value. Oh, by the way, I also purchase gas, and periodically other items, so who benefits with good coffee values?

Similarly, pop (soda) seems to have a value strictly based on demand. Most retail stores, it seems, price pop in a funny way. As an example, a can (12 oz.) of nationally known pop may run $1.00. A 20 oz. bottle may run $1.89, a one-liter bottle, $1.49 and a two-liter bottle on sale could run 99 cents! Where's the value? Where the money is being made!

The above point, based on what most retailers do, seems to say, "If you can make the money, get it!" At Bernie's, we felt it was much better to make a little bit on each bottle and to sell more. So, if we split up an eight pack of 16-ounce bottles of pop that may sell for 25 cents per bottle, we might have sold it cold for 35 cents. The hopes were that more people would purchase pop from Bernie's and that those people would purchase higher margin items, like cigarettes, snacks and candy, at the same time.

As a service item in itself, price isn't typically an issue, but I included it here because we felt that pricing fairly was an important trust issue with the customers. If customers make mistrust an issue with you, then all the great service in the world won't make up for that.

Does your place of business price products fairly? This is not to suggest that you break even or lose money on your products, because research has shown that customers do want you to make money, they just don't want to receive poor value or be priced inappropriately.

Staple #14: If you are going to do something, do it well.

"Serve the coldest beer and pop in town!"

Why does something if you are not going to do it right? Customer research showed that our customers wanted cold beer and pop. There was no way we were not going to do what our customers wanted, so we set the coolers at the coldest possible temperatures possible without freezing the drinks.

This was simply listening to what our customers wanted and responding to their needs. Although we stocked a wide variety of pop and beer, we didn't sell anything different than anyone else, so we did what we could—made it colder and therefore better. If it was a hot day or someone just wanted a cold drink, Bernie's is where they turned.

Isn't it an easy concept? If you want to be better than the competition, listen to what your customers want—then be better at it than your competition!

Frozen Foods

Can you think of a product that your business offers, or one offered by another business that might not be too easy to sell or profitable, but that the business might feel could be a good value for the customer? I can! How about old prepaid calling cards, which were a bit more expensive than direct dialing but offered convenience to the customers. Many businesses lost money by purchasing prepaid calling cards in advance, then finding customer enthusiasm not too great. Other examples are smart cards and the Edsel!

At Bernie's our product line was frozen foods. These often offered next-best-thing-to-fresh values for customers, but many frozen foods are difficult to sell because of the perceived look or quality They were high cost (maintaining and running the frozen food cases) and low turnover (didn't sell as fast as other items), which added up to low or no profit. To make a profit we had to improve efficiency and improve turnover. Efficiency was maintained by updating coolers periodically and by keeping the coolers in use running efficiently. The turnover was where customer service was extremely important. Customers, we found, simply weren't interested as much in the convenience that frozen offered which resulted in sales not being as high as in other departments.

Bernie felt frozen foods were a good value to customers. The food was often quite good, and prices were not out of line. So, we spent much of our promotional efforts marketing frozen foods to get those inventories to turn faster.

Staple #15: Find ways to explode myths or misperceptions about products.

"Frozen doesn't mean bad—give samples!"

Everyone loves ice cream, so selling ice cream was a piece of cake (pardon the pun). Frozen fruits, vegetables, dinners, meats, and more were another story! The perception that frozen was bad seemed to be a common one, and often times quite correct! Some of the frozen foods were horrible, but many were quite good.

So how does a business get its customers to try these items?

When Bernie's switched some of their popular fresh meat items to fresh frozen, customers hated the switch. This switch was definitely a mistake made without doing the proper research. It was convenient for the business but not for the customer. Customers thought they wanted fresh meats and we thought they wouldn't mind fresh frozen, which were every bit as good.

After the outcry, we went to work advertising the great taste. We advertised in the paper, put up signs, and put a grill in front of the store to grill up and give out samples. With the "after the switch" campaign, we found that many customers actually did like the high quality and better price that the frozen meats offered. Others still wanted fresh, so the store simply restocked the fresh meats and kept the frozen lines. Both enjoyed successes, but extra space was used by the store for the two product lines, yet total sales didn't change much.

The morals of this story are: If you are going to make a big change, ask your customers first; and if you make a change to provide customers with a better value, take into consideration the cost of educating your customers. It is often difficult to have our own staff make changes, let alone our customers. Educating them can be a long, expensive process.

Dad also used to say, "Don't be afraid to open a box."

There are as many different ice cream treats available as there are candy bars, and many of them have the same name. It seems as though once a month or so, there was a new product being offered as an ice cream treat. How do customers know what is what? How does the staff know what is what? If we are to be experts, we must know the product! So typically, if new products were offered, the staff tried them first. Either Bernie purchased them for us, or he requested that the vendor give out some samples to staff. And did we ever hate it when a new ice cream treat was introduced! "What, ice cream again?"

Also, as in the soda area, ice cream treat boxes were opened so customers could purchase individual items. This helped the lunch traffic as well as student purchases.

If you are involved in product introduction, you have got one great test market in your staff. Make sure they all know the product and those who want to might test it prior to public introduction. No one can sell a product that they don't know anything about.

Staple #16: Offer specials on new or low turnover items.

"The customer won't buy what they don't know!"

Because of the low frozen food's turnover, it was important to keep frozen foods in front of the customers' eyes. Bernie's always had a policy of pricing fairly on almost all products, with few specials. One exception was frozen foods. Specials were often run on various frozen food items so people would try them and incorporate them into their normal shopping trips. Specials were also often run on in-season produce.

If you want customers to know, you must let customers know. Not everyone knows the frozen foods section. Not everyone knows what produce is in season when. Specials are great for educating customers. In my opinion as a marketer for the past twenty years, marketing should be used to educate the customers, not to out-price the competition. When we use specials as a price tool, every business loses as competitors beat up on each other (gas price wars are a good example), and the customer never does learn about the products. Think of your marketing as ways of letting the customer know what you do and what you offer—not as a tool for crushing your across-the-street competitor on price. Value counts!

Consumer Packaged Goods

Consumer packaged goods. In essence, these are commodities. Every store offers canned goods, chips, cleaning supplies, cereal, sugar, salt, toilet paper, and soap. Most stores carry items that every household likely needs (although I did read not too long ago that 2% of households don't have televisions, which I can understand, and 2% of households don't have toilet paper. What do they use - sandpaper? Ouch!) There are minor differences in product names of these packaged goods and different stores stock new items at different times, but the major difference between stores is price.

Staple #17: More choices isn't always better—name brand and off brand.

"Salt is salt!"

Sometimes it is ridiculous seeing the different number of brands of coffee or toilet paper available. However, in the case of coffee or toilet paper, people often are fussy about which brand they use.

People tend to be less fussy about things like sugar, flour, raisins, soups, and more. Customer research showed that it did not really matter which brand of these types of items were stocked, as long as we stocked the items. So instead of taking up valuable room with a variety of choices, we typically offered one name brand and one-off brand—like our principal supplier's own name brand. This offered customers perceived high quality as well as perceived low cost.

Trying to be everything to everyone can be a very expensive proposition. Periodically, we would have requests for a specific brand that we didn't carry. If this happened, we had, at our discretion, the ability to give the customer a sample of an alternative product for them to test themselves. Sure, that strategy costs money, but it is a small marketing price to pay to gain or maintain a long-term customer.

There are two lessons to be learned by this staple. First, just because there are brands offered, you don't have to carry them all. How many automobile dealers do you know of that carry every brand of car? How many appliance stores carry every brand of major appliance? Obviously, these are extremes, as the costs would be very high (as well as regulatory problems.) The point is that it is not cost effective to carry everything. Can you cut down on brands without cutting down on service?

Staple #18: Convenience is valuable to customers.

"Make money on the stuff you can't compete on!"

Here's a total change of pace for me, and really not a customer service item. We, at Bernie's, decided that we could never and would never compete with the large pharmacies and discount stores in pharmaceutical prices (aspirin, Band-Aids, etc.). We were a small provider of these types of products, and we couldn't even purchase items for what some of the large stores were selling them for. Therefore, and this was the only area in which we did this, we maintained a minimal stock on a number of these types of items, and we priced them up. This was a key convenience area, which meant to us that someone might find convenience in picking up a bag of cough drops (for example) while grocery shopping versus going all the way to the discount store for the same item.

If your business offers a convenience item that you cannot compete with other stores on, do you try to compete anyway and cut your prices and profit, or do you increase the price and increase profits? You may want to think strategically about the products you sell and what your key products versus extras are. How do you want to price these items? Is it worth marketing them? Is it worth stocking them?

Convenience also is a key to getting and maintaining long term customers in other ways. At Bernie's besides needing boxes for packing up groceries for people, they were in high demand. Almost daily people asked for moving boxes. We were careful to open boxes neatly when we stocked shelves, to put aside the best boxes to pack groceries into, to throw out the bad boxes and to keep the rest in storage for those who wanted them.

Keeping boxes cost the store virtually nothing, as the room was available. Yet it was a valuable service to our customers.

We also provided other convenience items like postage stamps. These were sold to customers at no mark-up, for convenience only. Dad figured he had to go to the post office periodically anyway, so why not buy a few extra stamps for customers.

There ain't no such thing as a free lunch, right? What low or no cost service can you provide to your customers? Some hotels put out chocolates on pillows, some auto dealers add air fresheners when you purchase a car, some fast food restaurants leave coolers of water out for thirsty passers-by. These are commonly called value added services. They work particularly well if you are the first to provide them, because if they truly are value added, competition will catch on quickly and the services will become expected.

A few years ago, a discount hotel chain came up with the value-added service of offering coffee and donuts in the lobby as a continental breakfast for their guests. Now, most discount chains offer these breakfasts, and some have made them so extravagant that I suspect the costs are quite high. What value added services can you provide that make you a market leader?

Checkout

This chapter represents the final chapter in the supermarket layout. So far, the layout has focused on many "staples," but most of them have not been customer face-to-face service-related items. Checkout, to Bernie's, was the true key to success. Everything else was very important. Without the best customer service possible, meaning customer interaction throughout their shopping experience, the rest would not even exist.

The area of face-to-face customer service, in my opinion, is where many retail and other businesses fall short.

Recently, my wife and I went to a convenience store (one of a large chain) to buy a cup of iced cappuccino. We were amazed at the service we received. The customer service person, a woman who had "trainee" on her name tag, was the most pleasant we have encountered in a long time. She not only sold us the coffee, she told us how it was made, informed us how frequently they clean the machines, and gave us samples of another item to try, which we have since purchased. This is great service!

Often, customer service people are among the lowest tier on the pay scale. Does it make sense that key customer contact people—the ones who truly represent a business to the public, are the lowest paid and often lowest educated staff? I think a business who reconsiders this might truly benefit by having higher level, higher paid staff representing the business to the public.

Staple #19: People generally don't like lines, so work at being fast.

"Lines are for geometry, not the store!"

At the supermarket, people usually loved to take their time shopping. During the shopping experience, they would often chat about whatever came to their minds, ask questions about food items or simply stroll around the store. But when it came to checkout time, everyone wanted to get it done quickly! Now I'm not a psychologist, but I suppose there is some scientific reason why this occurs. Regardless, when we were checking customers out, we were fast.

Successful amusement parks and many businesses put a lot of time and effort into decreasing lines or making them move much more quickly. An amusement park in Minnesota used to have a log ride that seemed to take forever to get on. Recently, we went there. We entered the enclosed waiting area with no line, but soon found out they had expanded the inside waiting area to make it appear to be less of a line outside. We were horrified to think that we were now stuck inside waiting for the ride with no chance of escape! The better news soon followed, though. The park had also reworked the loading method on the ride to actually make the line move much more quickly. So our expected hour wait turned into a quick 15 minutes. What a pleasant surprise.

Fifteen minutes is unacceptable in most retail stores. The point is to work hard to exceed customer expectations for waiting.

The key to this staple is that it is so important to know the customer. When the customer wants something, don't make them wait, be fast and be accurate. At the bank, I used to ask the tellers to greet the customer at least five feet before they reached the window. Even if a teller was finishing up their last transaction, they were expected to greet the customer immediately (which let the customer know that he or she is important), then give them some kind of expectation like, "I'll be with you as soon as I finish this last transaction. It will only be a few seconds." Why did we emphasize this? Because the customer wanted it, and we didn't want the customer to be uncomfortable for even a tenth of a second.

Staple #20: Don't make cross selling a chore. It is as easy as a simple question to help the customer.

"Will there be anything else?!"

After we greeted the customer at the checkout, we always were required to ask, "Will there be anything else?" Notice, we did not say, "Will that be all?", or, "Is that it?" Bernie always felt that by asking either of those last two questions, it made it easy for the customer to simply say yes or that would be that. "Will there be anything else?" forces the customer to think about their needs, to check their lists, to ask questions if they couldn't find an item, and to not simply say yes.

This is a very simple cross sell technique. It is not in any way pushy or hard-selling—it is simply an easy customer service question that has a goal of making the customer think about their own needs. Periodically, we might add, "Did you remember the milk?" or, "would you be interested in such-and-such, which is on sale today?" We always felt that every additional purchase by a customer was satisfying for both the store and the customer.

Staple #21: Count the change back.

"Always count the change back—backwards!"

What would we do without computers today? Almost without exception, the computerized registers of today automatically calculate the change to be returned to the customer. Most people simply input your cash amount, let the machine calculate the change, then hand it back to you! This is not only slow, it allows checkout people an easy way to cheat the customer if they were so inclined, and is not at all customer friendly. Additionally, it allows customer service people to let their brains get a bit lazy, like our friend in Alaska who couldn't even subtract a dollar.

Think about this, in today's world of digital watches, how often do you hear it is a quarter to the hour or half past the hour anymore? People typically say it is 5:45 or 3:30! With the onset of computers and the decrease in reading, I think our minds and our children's' minds have gotten a bit too lazy.

At Bernie's, we took the cash from the customer, laid it on top of the register so the customer couldn't say they gave us a bigger bill, then were expected to quickly and easily count the change back, to the penny, to the customer. For example, if the total bill was $7.58 and the customer gave us a twenty, we would put the twenty on top, grab $12.42, and count it back from low to high—"$7.60, $7.65, $7.75, $8.00, nine, ten and twenty." After the customer was satisfied, we would put the twenty into the register. By using this method, the change was counted twice by us and once with the customer.

Customers don't like to be cheated or short changed, and I feel they prefer open honesty (counting money back) versus presumed honesty (handing back the change in a lump sum). This may be a minor detail, but gaining trust from people is important to any person or business, and losing trust is so easy to do, it seems. Why take the chance of making an error when you can prevent it with easy, quick steps? Oh, and by the way, we gave them their coins first, then the bills. There is no chance of the coins sliding off that way.

Staple #22: The customer is your reason for being, so let them know you appreciate their business.

"Thank you and come again!"

I always say thank you! As a customer, I say thank you to the clerk. As a businessperson, I always thank the customer and ask them back. How can you run a business and not tell the customer you appreciate their business and want them back?

As a customer, my pet peeve is that the clerks do not thank me and sometimes don't say anything. Without customers, they won't have a job. And if I say thank you, and they say, "no problem," that makes me suspect that there is a problem.

Although many people are politely taught to respond to "Thank you" with "You're welcome," I think it is important to always reply with, "Thank YOU!" In other words, the customer may or may not say thank you to the employee, but the employee must always thank the customer. Although it is a bit preachy, without the customer there wouldn't be an employee of that business!

As a customer, try saying, "thank you" the next few times you purchase something. See what response you receive.

Staple #23: Ask the customer if you can carry out the bags.

"Grab their bags and run!"

Customer service doesn't just stop at doing what is expected. It must include going beyond what is expected. I have done a number of talks regarding, "Shocking Service." This doesn't mean shocking on the negative side. What it does mean is that we must find ways to go over and above our average good service to shock the customer with excellent service. As I've alluded to however, it seems as though in today's world, good service is shocking enough!

Carrying out bags took just a few seconds for any customer who wanted it. We simply grabbed the bags, walked out to the customer's car, and placed the bags wherever the customer wanted them. It was easy, quick, and customers loved the service.

What can you do in your personal or business life to provide shocking service to people? How can you be a little bit better than expectations? How can you be a lot better than your competition?

Paper or Plastic?

"Wrapping it all up."

Twenty-three staples for a small business, and many more that were led by example (as were all of the staples). These are no secrets or mysteries. They are the keys to staying competitive years ago, and the methods for getting ahead in today's world of forgotten customer service skills.

The staples laid out in this book may or may not all apply to you. And there are thousands of more staples from other areas of business and life that you encounter every day. Pay attention to the details, and learn how to improve yourself and your business. Every day, I work at noticing the great service skills that people offer.

But regardless of how many staples you come up with, or how you use them, as a business, remember Staple #1—The Customer is Always Right! This was our mission, our theme, our reason for being. Dad never, ever let us forget this staple. And, profitable or not, it was rule number one when considering the other staples.

There were a few other interesting quotes from dad that we followed that might be of interest:

"Drive the car to work!"

Dad didn't make us drive a car to work because he was lazy. We only lived three blocks away, and we were all pretty athletic and could easily have sprinted that far (in fact, we did once in a while for emergencies!) The idea behind this staple is image. Dad never wanted the store to look deserted or empty. His thoughts were that a person driving by would rather pull into a store with others present than to drive into an empty one.

In the same way, I remember traveling in the car, and my folks would only stop at the truck stops where there were many trucks parked. They always figured that if the truckers stopped there, they must be good. If not, forget it!

If I may paraphrase my friend Dan Hegstad— in one of his speeches, he says, "Thinking, acting, and feeling are a three-legged stool— we can't change one without affecting the other two directly. So if you act happy and positive, you must, by definition, think positive thoughts and feel happy and positive. It is impossible to not be that way." I think this is the root to having the car in front of the store. If we acted like there were people there and we were busy, then we would necessarily be busier and enjoy work more.

Do you drive your car to work? At work, are things the way they are because you want to succeed or because you want to fail? Is your desk messy because you are too busy for customers or because you want more customers? Are you and others happy at work, or just there because you have to be? Think about your image and what you really want to achieve.

"Answer the phone: Good Morning (Afternoon, Evening) Bernie's! How can I help you?!"

For any business, every telephone call is a potential sale. Dad was particular about how we answered the phone. You may have heard the expression, "You never get a second chance to make a first impression!" At Bernie's, the thought was that everyone who called in was either a potential customer, a salesperson, a potential customer, a friend or family member, a potential customer or a wrong number (potential customer?)! By identifying the store in a pleasant manner, then seeing to the potential customer's needs, you got right to the point with this answer. We were always to be polite, even if very busy.

What percentage of your customers or potential customers use the phone? How do you answer it?

I will never forget the time I called a business for the first time, and they answered, "It's a Great Day at Marquis! How can I help make yours even better?!" Wow! I used to call them periodically just to hear them answer the phone! By the way, this was also one of the best companies I have ever dealt with from a service standpoint! The way they answered their phones was directly correlated to their service.

One final thing about phones—in the supermarket, we didn't have automatic voice response units. My feeling is that a company who has a choice, and who uses live people to answer the phones and direct your calls, is far superior from a customer service standpoint over those who have a machine answer.

"Treat the customer as you want to be treated!"

Related to, and almost as important as "The Customer is Always Right" is this quote: Call it the golden rule or whatever you'd like, it is so important to put yourself in the customer's shoes before reacting to a situation.

Once a man came into the store to purchase an eight pack of soda. This man was a bit unsteady on his feet, and he stumbled as he headed toward the cooler. As most people do, he reacted by grabbing the closest thing to him, which happened to be a whole stack of eight packs, that tumbled over and broke all over the place!

Thank goodness the customer didn't get hurt, which was always our first concern. But after checking that, Dad could have reacted by scolding the customer, charging him for all of the soda, and telling him never to set foot in the store again.

The customer already felt horrible, and was very apologetic, saying he would pay for the broken bottles. Dad told him to forget it, that accidents happen and that it was forgotten with no mention of it ever again. This was immeasurable service and even better word of mouth advertising. Bernie had just made a lifelong customer!

Summary

I hope you've enjoyed this book on Supermarket Service and can take with you a few ideas for your personal life or business. Now work on making changes to how you act and work. If true customer service is achieved, success will come your way!

Here is an overview of the staples that we have discussed. Prioritize them in accordance with your needs (personally or in the business), and start working on the most needed skills first.

Staple to Live By

Staple #1: The Customer is Always Right

Even if the customer isn't always right, the customer is always right.

Face to Face Service Staples

These staples are ideas for how to improve customer service and to make the customer the focus of your day.

Staple #9: Listen to every customer.

The best salespeople listen more than they talk.

Staple #19: People generally don't like lines, so work at being fast.

The customer wants competent, speedy service, so give the customer competent, speedy service.

Staple #20: Don't make cross selling a chore. It's as easy as a simple question to help the customer.

Employees like to do what is easy, fun and helpful to others.

Staple #21: Count the change back.

Machines are great, but at the expense of employee minds and customer trust?

Staple #22: The customer is your reason for being, so let them know you appreciate their business.

Take "You're welcome" out of your customer service vocabulary.

Product Staples

Product offerings, presentation, inventory levels and choice are important to your customers. Make sure you offer what the customer wants -

not necessarily what management feels is the best.

Staple #3: Make what is truly unique your showpiece.

Become known for your niche specialties.

Staple #4: Personalize your service to the extent possible.

Making your customers feel special as individuals helps make you special in their eyes.

Staple #11: Check your inventory regularly for defects or wear.

Make Murphy's Law a non-issue. Check before the customer does.

Staple #12: If selection is important to your customers, be "top of mind" by providing the largest selection.

Give customers a reason to come to the store.

Staple #15: Find ways to explode myths or misperceptions about products.

Educating customers can work in your favor.

Staple #17: More choices isn't always better - name brand and off brand.

You can't afford to be everything to everyone.

Pricing Staples

Offering good values, making money and serving the customer in the best way possible is what it is all about.

Staple #6: Become known for providing a good value to the customer.

Perceived value is more important than price alone.

Staple #13: Price fairly.

Even the best service in the world won't overcome prices that are way too high.

Staple #16: Offer specials on new or low turnover items.

Random specials don't work—use strategy when offering them.

Customer Viewpoint Staples

Looking through the customer's eyes is something we often forget to do, or don't have time for. Every single customer does, though! Even personally, does your car or home present itself the way you want others to see it?

Staple #7: Make your products appealing to the customer.

The better they look, the better they appeal to the customers.

Staple #10: The best ways to sell more of a commodity is to be better liked or to provide a better presentation.

Paying attention to the details can go a long way.

Staple #18: Convenience is Valuable to Customers.

How can you beat the competition and still make a living?

Staple #23: Ask the customer if you can carry out the bags.

A little extra effort can go a long way.

The Necessities

These need not even be mentioned, because they are like our mothers telling us to brush our teeth or wash before meals.

Staple #2: Enjoy what you do, and let it show through to the customer from the time they set foot in the door.

Life is too short and special to not enjoy every second.

Staple #5: Cleanliness is all about business integrity.

If you are going to err, err on the side of being "too" clean.

Staple #8: Be the expert on your products and the competition.

Your customer expects you to know the product, and knowing the competitors' products is a bonus.

Staple #14: If you are going to do something, do it well.

Half-hearted means half the sales.

Closing Stories

Thank you so much for reading this book. I hope you were able to get some good information! And when I write my next, please come again!

When you are in any business for many years, there are a few good little
anecdotes that come along. Here are a few that I remember that I hope you enjoy!

The Downhill Parking Lot!

Bernie's parking lot, because of the way it was situated on the road, peaked right in the center and was downhill going north and southeast. North was a lightly used residential street, and Southeast, just in front of the store was a busy road that was one of the main roads in the city.

The parking lot never tended to be a problem, but periodically brakes weren't properly set.

Once, I was working and a man came in saying, "Say, I just saw a tractor going down the street and no one was driving it!" I ran out the door and there went a city tractor! One of the workers had stopped into the store to get lunch. He improperly set the brake on the tractor. It had rolled down the North side of the lot onto the residential street and was slowly moving down the right side of the street, just as if it were being driven! Unfortunately, the ghost driver couldn't avoid the parked car down the road and some damage was done.

We had many close calls over the slanted parking lot. But it sure did make a great conversation piece!

The Robberies

In all the years we were open, we only had two armed robberies. There were a few break-ins during the night, but only two occurred when the store was open.

Once my grandmother was working the checkout counter. Now, grandma was all of five feet, if that (and I believe she was the tallest of the four sisters!). She weighed in back then at just over 100 pounds, talked with her eastern European accent that she still had from when she came to the U.S. as a young child, and was probably around 65 or 70 years old. She had a full head of orange hair and was about as stereotypical of a grandmother as possible. She was and is a very beautiful, nice woman and would never harm anyone or anything.

One bright sunny day, a man came in with a mask on, walked to the checkout desk, held up a weapon and demanded that my grandmother open the till and get down on the floor.

Grandma said, "I'm not about to get dirty! You can have the money if you want, but I am not going to lie down on the filthy floor!" This frustrated the would-be thief, and he ran out of the store with nothing! The day my 100-pound grandmother defeated the thief!

Another time, Dad was working alone at the store. Again, a thief came in, held his hand in his pocket with something pointing out, and told Dad he had a gun and wanted all of the money.

My father, who is quite jovial and outgoing, decided he would talk to the thief for a while. So he did! He eventually got him to the front door and told the thief that he could shoot him (Dad) if he wanted to, but they were already outside and he would get no money. The thief got into his car and took off. A customer coming up to the store saw this last part and followed the thief. He got his license number, stopped and called the police (no cell phones back then!), and they quickly apprehended the thief.

The police soon called the store and told Dad that they had bagged the criminal—gun and all! The police yelled at Dad for trying to be a hero, and I recall my mother not being very happy either!

The Bagel

Nowadays, it seems as though there is a bagel shop on every street corner. Back when Bernie's was doing business, there were very few to be found. But being in the grocery business, you never knew when a new line of bagels might pop up.

I was young and working with Dad one Saturday. In came a customer with a newly weaned puppy that his beagle had mothered. It was half beagle and half mountain lion, as we always used to say! Dad called home and asked mom if she wanted him to bring home a beagle. She said, "Sure!"

Well, to my mother's surprise, we walked in with this tiny little beagle puppy, and mom said, "I thought you asked if you should bring home bagels!" Our new puppy, Bagel, became part of the family for many years to come!

Laugh. Love. Learn. Teach

www.ingramcontent.com/pod-product-compliance
Lightning Source LLC
Chambersburg PA
CBHW071415210526
45465CB00001B/400